# Hot Math Topics

### Problem Solving, Communication, and Reasoning

# Decimals and Fractions

FISH FOOD

$\frac{1}{4}$ lb cod........$3.99
$\frac{1}{3}$ lb sole........$6.99
1 lb clams....$12.99

grade
4

**Carole Greenes**
**Linda Schulman Dacey**
**Rika Spungin**

Dale Seymour Publications®

**Acknowledgement:** The authors wish to acknowledge the outstanding contributions of Mali Apple in the production of the *Hot Math Topics* series. She has given careful attention to the content, design, and art, and helped shepherd the program through from its inception to its completion. Thank you, Mali.

Editorial Manager: Carolyn Coyle
Project Editor: Mali Apple
Production/Manufacturing Director: Janet Yearian
Production/Manufacturing Manager: Karen Edmonds
Senior Production/Manufacturing Coordinator: Roxanne Knoll
Art Director: Jim O'Shea
Cover Design: Tracey Munz
Cover and Interior Illustrations: Jared Lee
Computer Graphics: Alan Noyes

ISBN 0-7690-0837-2
Printed in the United States of America
2 3 4 5 6 7 8 9 10      07 06 05 04 03

Dale
Seymour
Publications

Pearson Learning Group

1-800-321-3106
www.pearsonlearning.com

# contents

# Introduction

## Why Was *Hot Math Topics* Developed?

The *Hot Math Topics* series was developed for several reasons:

- to offer students practice and maintenance of previously learned skills and concepts
- to enhance problem solving and mathematical reasoning abilities
- to build literacy skills
- to nurture collaborative learning behaviors

### Practicing and maintaining concepts and skills

Although textbooks and core curriculum materials do treat the topics explored in this series, their treatment is often limited by the lesson format and the page size. As a consequence, there are often not enough opportunities for students to practice newly acquired concepts and skills related to the topics, or to connect the topics to other content areas. *Hot Math Topics* provides the necessary practice and mathematical connections.

Similarly, core instructional programs often do not do a very good job of helping students maintain their skills. Although textbooks do include reviews of previously learned material, they are frequently limited to sidebars or boxed-off areas on one or two pages in each chapter, with four or five exercises in each box. Each set of problems is intended only as a sampling of previously taught topics, rather than as a complete review. In the selection and placement of the review exercises, little or no attention is given to levels of complexity of the problems. By contrast, *Hot Math Topics* targets specific topics and gives students more experience with concepts and skills related to them. The problems are sequenced by difficulty, allowing students to hone their skills. And, because they are not tied to specific lessons, the problems can be used at any time.

### Enhancing problem solving and mathematical reasoning abilities

*Hot Math Topics* presents students with situations in which they may use a variety of problem solving strategies, including

- designing and conducting experiments to generate or collect data
- guessing, checking, and revising guesses
- organizing data in lists or tables in order to identify patterns and relationships
- choosing appropriate computational algorithms and deciding on a sequence of computations
- using inverse operations in "work backward" solution paths

For their solutions, students are also required to bring to bear various methods of reasoning, including

- deductive reasoning
- inductive reasoning
- proportional reasoning

For example, to solve clue-type problems, students must reason deductively and make inferences about mathematical relationships in order to generate candidates for the solutions and to hone in on those that meet all of the problem's conditions.

To identify and continue a pattern and then write a rule for finding the next term in that pattern, students must reason inductively.

To compute unit prices and generate equivalent fractions, students must reason proportionally.

To estimate or compare decimals and fractions, students must apply their number sense skills.

### Building communication and literacy skills

*Hot Math Topics* offers students opportunities to write and talk about mathematical ideas. For many problems, students must describe their solution paths, justify their solutions, give their opinions, or write or tell stories.

Some problems have multiple solution methods. With these problems, students may have to compare their methods with those of their peers and talk about how their approaches are alike and different.

Other problems have multiple solutions, requiring students to confer to be sure they have found all possible answers.

### Nurturing collaborative learning behaviors

Several of the problems can be solved by students working together. Some are designed specifically as partner problems. By working collaboratively, students can develop expertise in posing questions that call for clarification or verification, brainstorming solution strategies, and following another person's line of reasoning.

## What Is in *Decimals and Fractions?*

This book contains 100 problems and tasks: 50 involve primarily decimals and 50 involve primarily fractions; a few involve both. The mathematics content, the mathematical connections, the problem solving strategies, and the communication skills that are emphasized are described below.

### Mathematics content

The decimal problems and tasks require students to

- identify decimals on a number line
- compare, order, and compute with decimals
- understand place value to thousandths
- estimate sums and products
- compute means
- compare fractions to decimals

The fraction problems and tasks require students to

- identify fractions on a number line
- identify equivalent fractions
- identify the fractional part of a discrete set and the fractional part of a whole
- compare and order fractions
- identify fractions between two given fractions
- convert improper fractions to mixed numbers and vice versa
- compute with fractions and mixed numbers

### Mathematical connections

In these problems and tasks, connections are made to these other topic areas:

- algebra
- geometry
- measurement
- graphs
- statistics

## Problem solving strategies

*Decimals and Fractions* problems and tasks offer students opportunities to use one or more of several problem solving strategies.

- **Formulate Questions:** When data are presented in displays or text form, students must pose one or more questions that can be answered using the given data.

- **Complete Stories:** When confronted with an incomplete story, students must supply the missing information and then check that the story makes sense.

- **Organize Information:** To ensure that several solution candidates for a problem are considered, students may have to organize information by using a picture, list, diagram, or table.

- **Guess, Check, and Revise:** In some problems, students have to identify candidates for the solution and then check whether those candidates match the conditions of the problem. If the conditions are not satisfied, other possible solutions must be generated and verified.

- **Identify and Continue Patterns:** To identify the next term or terms in a sequence, students have to recognize the relationship between successive terms and then generalize that relationship.

- **Use Logic:** Students have to reason deductively, from clues, to make inferences about the solution to a problem. They must reason proportionally to determine which of two buys is better. They have to reason inductively to continue numeric patterns.

- **Work Backward:** In some problems, the output is given and students must determine the input by identifying mathematical relationships between the input and output and applying inverse operations.

## Communication skills

Problems and tasks in *Decimals and Fractions* are designed to stimulate communication. As part of the solution process, students may have to

- describe their thinking steps
- provide a mathematical explanation
- describe patterns and rules
- find alternate solution methods and solution paths
- identify other possible answers
- formulate problems for classmates to solve
- compare solutions and methods with classmates

These communication skills are enhanced when students interact with one another and with the teacher. By communicating both orally and in writing, students develop their understanding and use of the language of mathematics.

## How Can *Hot Math Topics* Be Used?

The problems may be used as practice of newly learned concepts and skills, as maintenance of previously learned ideas, and as enrichment experiences for early finishers or more advanced students.

They may be used in class or assigned for homework. If used during class, they may be selected to complement lessons dealing with a specific topic or assigned every week as a means of keeping skills alive and well. Because the problems often require the application of various problem solving strategies and reasoning methods, they may also form the basis of whole-class lessons whose goals are to develop expertise with specific problem solving strategies or methods.

The problems may be used by students working in pairs or on their own. Within each topic—*decimals* and *fractions*—the problems are sequenced from least to most difficult. The selection of problems may be made by the teacher or the students based on their needs or interests. If the plan is for students to choose problems, you may wish to copy individual problems onto card stock and laminate them, and establish a problem card file.

To facilitate record keeping, a Management Chart is provided on page 6. The chart can be duplicated so that there is one for each student. As a problem is completed, the space corresponding to that problem's number may be shaded. An Award Certificate is included on page 6 as well.

## How Can Student Performance Be Assessed?

*Decimals and Fractions* problems and tasks provide you with opportunities to assess students'

- knowledge of decimals and fractions
- problem solving abilities

- mathematical reasoning methods
- communication skills

### Observations

Keeping anecdotal records helps you to remember important information you gain as you observe students at work. To make observations more manageable, limit each observation to a group of from four to six students or to one of the areas noted above. You may find that using index cards facilitates the recording process.

### Discussions

Many of the *Decimals and Fractions* problems and tasks allow for multiple answers or may be solved in a variety of ways. This built-in richness motivates students to discuss their work with one another. Small groups or class discussions are appropriate. As students share their approaches to the problems, you will gain additional insights into their content knowledge, mathematical reasoning, and communication abilities.

### Scoring responses

You may wish to holistically score students' responses to the problems and tasks. The simple scoring rubric below uses three levels: high, medium, and low.

| High | Medium | Low |
|------|--------|-----|
| • Solution demonstrates that the student knows the concepts and skills. | • Solution demonstrates that the student has some knowledge of the concepts and skills. | • Solution shows that the student has little or no grasp of the concepts and skills. |
| • Solution is complete and thorough. | • Solution is complete. | • Solution is incomplete or contains major errors. |
| • Student communicates effectively. | • Student communicates somewhat clearly. | • Student does not communicate effectively. |

### Portfolios

Having students store their responses to the problems in *Hot Math Topics* portfolios allows them to see improvement in their work over time. You may want to have them choose examples of their best responses for inclusion in their permanent portfolios, accompanied by explanations as to why each was chosen.

### Students and the assessment process

Involving students in the assessment process is central to the development of their abilities to reflect on their own work, to understand the assessment standards to which they are held accountable, and to take ownership for their own learning. Young children may find the reflective process difficult, but with your coaching, they can develop such skills.

Discussion may be needed to help students better understand your standards for performance. Ask students such questions as, "What does it mean to communicate *clearly*?" "What is a *complete* response?" Some students may want to use the high-medium-low rubric to score their responses.

Participation in peer-assessment tasks will also help students to better understand the performance standards. In pairs or small groups, students can review each other's responses and offer feedback. Opportunities to revise work may then be given.

## What Additional Materials Are Needed?

One task requires pennies; two require crayons. No other special materials are needed for solving the problems in *Decimals and Fractions*. However, if they are available, decimal models (such as base ten blocks and decimal squares), fraction models (such as pattern blocks and fraction strips and bars), and calculators may be useful for some students in solving some of the problems.

## Management Chart

Name _____

When a problem or task is completed, shade the box with that number.

| 1 | 2 | 3 | 4 | 5 | 6 | 7 | 8 | 9 | 10 |
|---|---|---|---|---|---|---|---|---|----|
| 11 | 12 | 13 | 14 | 15 | 16 | 17 | 18 | 19 | 20 |
| 21 | 22 | 23 | 24 | 25 | 26 | 27 | 28 | 29 | 30 |
| 31 | 32 | 33 | 34 | 35 | 36 | 37 | 38 | 39 | 40 |
| 41 | 42 | 43 | 44 | 45 | 46 | 47 | 48 | 49 | 50 |
| 51 | 52 | 53 | 54 | 55 | 56 | 57 | 58 | 59 | 60 |
| 61 | 62 | 63 | 64 | 65 | 66 | 67 | 68 | 69 | 70 |
| 71 | 72 | 73 | 74 | 75 | 76 | 77 | 78 | 79 | 80 |
| 81 | 82 | 83 | 84 | 85 | 86 | 87 | 88 | 89 | 90 |
| 91 | 92 | 93 | 94 | 95 | 96 | 97 | 98 | 99 | 100 |

## Award Certificate

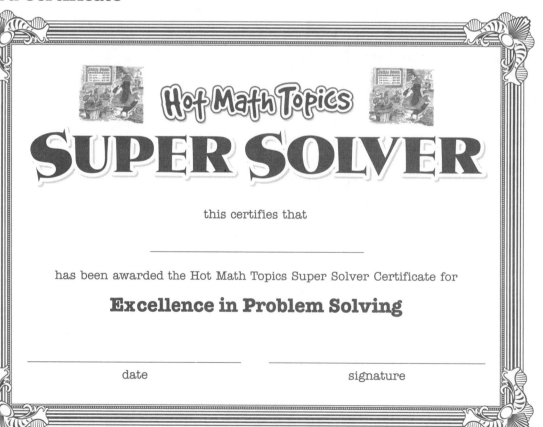

Hot Math Topics

# SUPER SOLVER

this certifies that

_____

has been awarded the Hot Math Topics Super Solver Certificate for

**Excellence in Problem Solving**

_____        _____
date                              signature

# Problems
# and Tasks

FISH FOOD

$\frac{1}{4}$ lb cod........$3.99
$\frac{1}{2}$ lb sole........$6.99
1 lb clams....$12.99

**Put numbers in the** 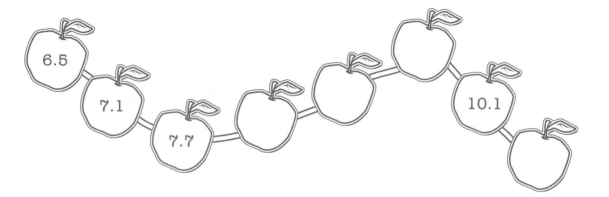 **to complete the pattern.**

6.5   7.1   7.7   ·   ·   ·   ·   10.1   ·

**Describe the pattern.**

----

**Match each decimal in the flower to a point on the number line.**

- Point *R* is ____.
- Point *S* is ____.
- Point *T* is ____.
- Point *U* is ____.
- Point *V* is ____.

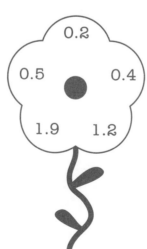

0.2   0.5   0.4   1.9   1.2

**Skating Scores**

| | |
|---|---|
| 5.8 | 4.2 |
| 6.0 | 4.9 |

**Miki's score is 0.9 greater than Leah's score.**

**Kim's score is 1.8 greater than Craig's score.**

**Tell the score of each skater.**

Miki's score: _____     Leah's score: _____

Kim's score: _____     Craig's score: _____

**In Waterville, it rained 2.34 inches on Monday, 4.6 inches on Tuesday, and 3.05 inches on Wednesday.**

**Waterville has a record of 11 inches of rain in 4 days.**

**How much does it have to rain on Thursday to break the record?**

**5**

I don't know whether 2.9 or 2.09 is greater.

2.9
2.09

**What could you draw and say to help the penguin know which number is greater?**

---

**6**

**The large square is made of 100 small squares.**

- Color 0.34 of the large square red.
- Color 0.20 of the large square yellow.
- Color 0.06 of the large square blue.
- Color the remainder of the large square green.

**What decimal represents the part of the large square that is green?**

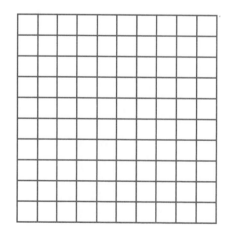

**During 6 weeks this summer, Nathan did yard work 2.5 hours every day, Monday through Thursday.**

**He earned $5 an hour.**

**How much money did Nathan earn?**

---

1.5  1.6  0.3  1.71

**Which decimal does not belong with the others?**

**Why?**

**Cross it out.**

**Write a new decimal in its place.**

**Compare your answer with a classmate's answer.**

Tomas measured the height of a plant at the end of each week.

### Plant Growth

| End of Week | Height in cm |
|:---:|:---:|
| 1 | 0.5 |
| 2 | 2.3 |
| 3 | 5.8 |
| 4 | 6.7 |
| 5 | 7.8 |

During which week did the plant grow the most?

How much did it grow that week?

- - - - - - - - - - - - - - - - - - - - - - - - - - - - - - - - - - - - - -

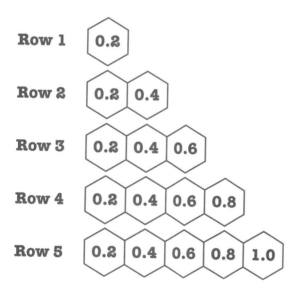

Row 1  0.2

Row 2  0.2  0.4

Row 3  0.2  0.4  0.6

Row 4  0.2  0.4  0.6  0.8

Row 5  0.2  0.4  0.6  0.8  1.0

The pattern continues.

What is the last number in row 9?

**The mystery number is on the sign.**

**Find the number.**

- The tenths digit is greater than 0.
- The ones digit is greater than the tens digit.
- The hundredths digit is 1 less than the hundreds digit.

**The number is _____ .**

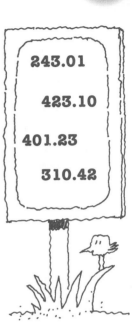

243.01

423.10

401.23

310.42

11

- - - - - - - - - - - - - - - - - - - - - - - - - - - - - - - - - - - - - -

12

$\triangle = 2.9$

$\square + \triangle = 3.4$

$\square + \triangle + \triangle = \underline{\quad}$

$\square + \square + \square + \triangle = \underline{\quad}$

**Find a set of 6 decimals that satisfies the clues.**

Four of the decimals are less than 1.6.

Four of the decimals have an even digit in the tenths place.

**Compare your set of 6 decimals with a classmate's set.**

- - - - - - - - - - - - - - - - - - - - - - - - - - - - - - - - - - - - - - - - - - - - - -

**Add across.**

**Add down.**

**The numbers in the circles are the sums.**

**Complete the grid.**

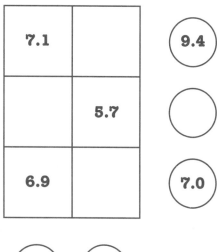

## What is the round-trip distance from Barrington to Saugus by way of Holland?

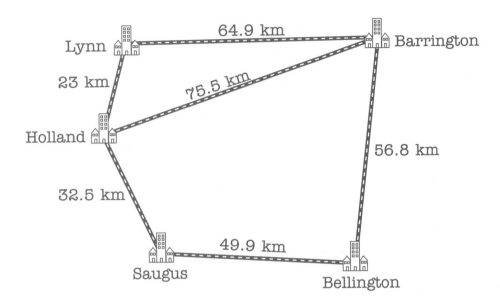

Lynn ————— 64.9 km ————— Barrington

23 km

75.5 km

Holland

56.8 km

32.5 km

Saugus ————— 49.9 km ————— Bellington

---

## Estimate to decide if you can buy 3 bags of chips and 2 granola bars for $8.

## Explain your thinking.

**Snacks**

Peanuts $1.45

Chips $.89

Apple $.75

Granola bar $1.75

**Joy, Mai, Nita, and Sean were in a walk-a-thon.**

- Joy said, "If I'd walked 0.6 mile more, I would have walked 3 miles."

- Mai said, "I didn't walk the shortest distance."

- Sean said, "I walked 0.9 mile more than Nita."

**Write the name next to the bar that gives the distance each student walked.**

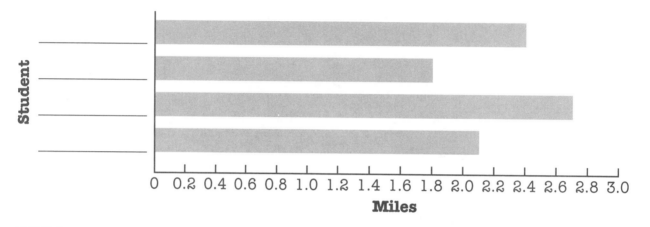

---

**The pattern continues for 30 terms.**

**Which terms between term 2 and term 25 have a 4 in the tenths place?**

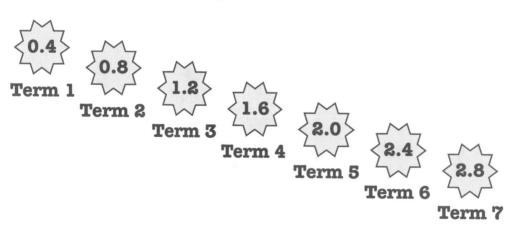

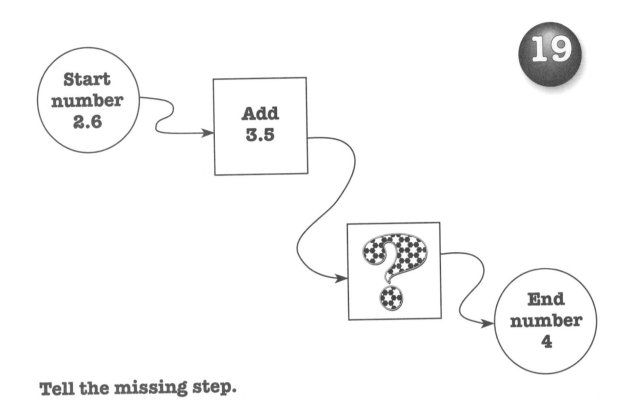

**19**

Tell the missing step.

- - - - - - - - - - - - - - - - - - - - - - - - - - - - - - - - - - - - - - - - - - - -

**20**

Play this game with a friend. Take turns.

Use 2 crayons of different colors.

On your turn:

• Choose 2 numbers from the sign and add them.

• Mark the sum on the game board.

The first player to get 4 in a row, column, or diagonal wins.

**Game Board**

| 7.56 | 4.75 | 3.20 | 1.55 |
|------|------|------|------|
| 5.65 | 4.0  | 4.05 | 5.11 |
| 2.4  | 5.96 | 5.6  | 2.45 |
| 1.19 | 4.36 | 3.15 | 6.01 |

**Put each digit from the sign into a square below.**

**Complete the subtraction problem.**

$$\boxed{\phantom{0}}.\boxed{\phantom{0}}\boxed{\phantom{0}}$$
$$-\boxed{\phantom{0}}.\boxed{\phantom{0}}\boxed{\phantom{0}}$$

5 . 0 9

---

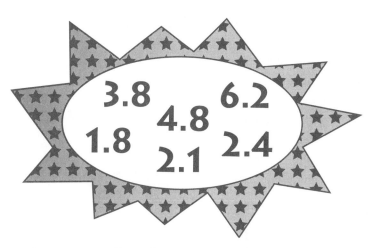

**The mystery number is on the sign.**

- It is greater than 2.2 − 0.3.
- It is less than 3.8 + 1.7.
- The ones digit is half of the tenths digit.
- The number plus 0.2 equals a whole number.

**What is the mystery number?**

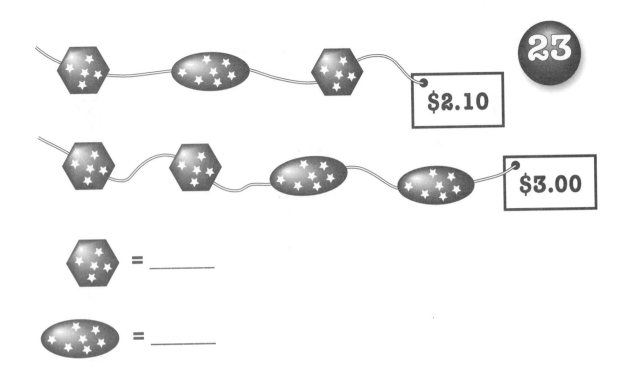

**23**

**24**

**Write a decimal number in tenths, hundredths, or thousandths that is between**

- 4 and 5
- 3 and 3.4
- 2 and 2.4
- 1 and 1.3
- 0 and 0.2

**Decimals and Fractions 19**

The judges gave Jackie's dive these scores:

**25**

7.8    8.5    8.1

7.5    9.0    7.6

To find her total score, the lowest and highest scores are eliminated.

The remaining scores are averaged.

What is Jackie's final score?

- - - - - - - - - - - - - - - - - - - - - - - - - - - - - - - - - - -

Ms. Shah bought tickets 1 through 10 on this roll.

**26**

The winning ticket was numbered 4.5.

Did Ms. Shah buy the winning ticket?

How do you know?

School Raffle ☆
You Could Win a CD Player
Tickets: 25¢ each
5 for $1.00

Ticket 1 — 1.2    Ticket 2 — 1.5    Ticket 3 — 1.8    Ticket 4 — 2.1    Ticket 5 — 2.4

**Record each number from the sign in the diagram below.**

**Put each number where it belongs.**

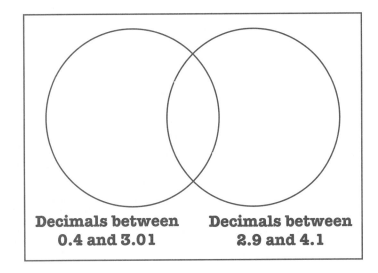

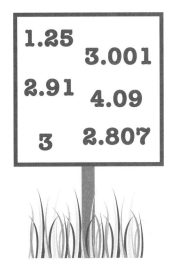

Decimals between 0.4 and 3.01

Decimals between 2.9 and 4.1

1.25    3.001
2.91    4.09
3    2.807

----

**Ring two numbers in each box.**

**Their sum must be in the range.**

2.459    6.78
12.72    14.84
9.71

**Range: 17–18**

68.4    12.7
36.6    42.9
57.6

**Range: 90–100**

4.01    0.4
3.02    1.67
0.75

**Range: 1–2**

**Use the facts.**

**Which letter represents which number from the mailbox?**

**Facts**

- A > C

- B < C

- D > A

A = _____   B = _____

C = _____   D = _____

---

**Eric and Kiran went on a bike tour.**

- They rode 8.4 miles before lunch.

- They rode twice as many miles after lunch.

**How many miles did they ride in all?**

**Each sphere weighs 5.4 ounces.**

**How many ounces does each pyramid weigh?**

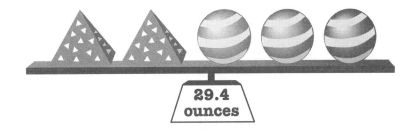

**Tell the steps you used to find the weight.**

- - - - - - - - - - - - - - - - - - - - - - - - - - - - - - - -

**The Radio News Show starts at 7:05 P.M.**

**What time does the show end?**

**Fill in the blanks.**

**Use the numbers shown.**

**The story must make sense.**

The race was _____ miles long.

Mario walked _____ miles, more than half of the total distance, before he stopped.

He stopped _____ miles before the finish line.

Clara, the winner, finished the race in _____ hours.

Vida finished last. She took _____ hours to finish the race.

3.6    2.25

4.25    6.5

2.1

---

**Use the digits 2, 4, and 5 to create 6 different numbers.**

**Use each digit in every number.**

**Then order your numbers from least to greatest.**

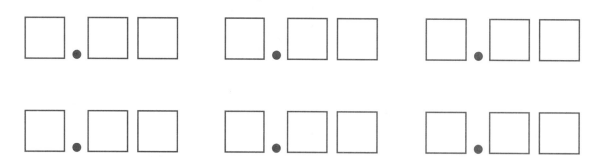

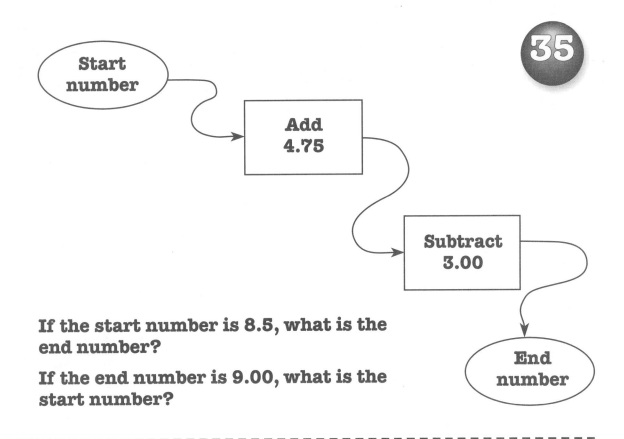

**35**

If the start number is 8.5, what is the end number?

If the end number is 9.00, what is the start number?

- - - - - - - - - - - - - - - - - - - - - - - - - - - - - - - - - - - -

**36**

Place a decimal point in each addend to make the sums true.

$$1\ 2\ 4\ 5 + 3\ 2\ 1 = 15.66$$

$$4\ 5\ 7 + 3\ 4\ 3 = 8$$

Add across. Add down.

The numbers in the circles are the sums.

Complete the grid.

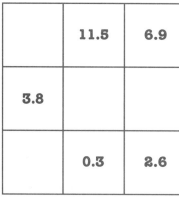

|  | 11.5 | 6.9 | (19.3) |
| 3.8 |  |  | (20.9) |
|  | 0.3 | 2.6 | ( ) |
| (10.9) | (21.5) | ( ) |  |

---

| **A** | **B** |
| 3.72 | 3.72 |
| −2.36 | −2.56 |

You can use the answer to A to find the answer to B. Explain how.

**A block of clay weighs 12 ounces.**

**It is cut as shown below.**

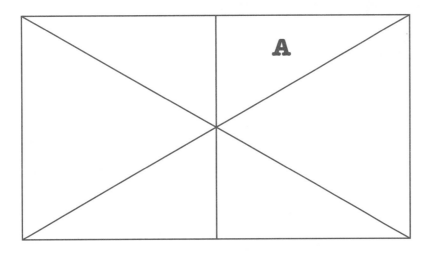

**What does piece A weigh?**

- - - - - - - - - - - - - - - - - - - - - - - - - - - - - - - - - - - - -

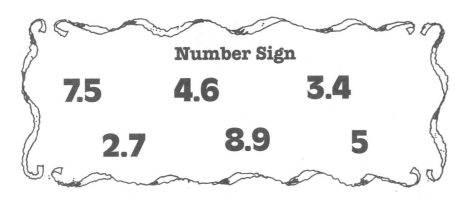

Number Sign

7.5     4.6     3.4

2.7     8.9     5

**Use each number on the sign once to make the number sentences true.**

$$\boxed{\phantom{xx}} + \boxed{\phantom{xx}} = 12.3$$

$$\boxed{\phantom{xx}} - \boxed{\phantom{xx}} = 4.8$$

$$\boxed{\phantom{xx}} \times \boxed{\phantom{xx}} = 23$$

Jahmal went from Gold City to Tintown to Silver Grove, a total of 32.1 km.

Emily drove from Tintown to Bronzeville to Silver Grove and back to Tintown, a total of 42.7 km.

How much farther is it from Tintown to Gold City than from Tintown to Bronzeville?

© Dale Seymour Publications®

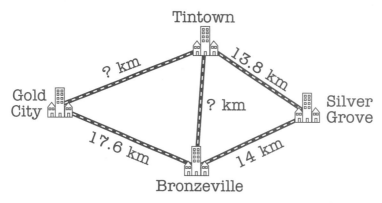

Make up another question about the map.

Answer your question.

- - - - - - - - - - - - - - - - - - - - - - - - - - - - - - - - - - - - - - - - - - - - - - - - - -

The perimeter of a rectangle is 29.2 centimeters.

The rectangle's length is 11.4 centimeters.

What is the width of the rectangle?

© Dale Seymour Publications®

**43**

Use all of the digits from the sign.

Put the digits in the squares so the statement is true.

Can you do it another way?

- - - - - - - - - - - - - - - - - - - - - - - - - - - - - - - - - - - - - - - - - - - - - - - - -

**44**

What is the *greatest* number you can think of that, when rounded to the nearest whole number, rounds to 4?

What is the *least* number you can think of that, when rounded to the nearest whole number, rounds to 4?

**Compare your answers with a friend.**

**The pattern continues.**

**What is the first number in row 21?**

**Tell how you know.**

| | | | |
|---|---|---|---|
| Row 1 | 0.5 / 1.0 / 1.5 / 2.0 |
| Row 2 | 2.5 \ 3.0 \ 3.5 \ 4.0 |
| Row 3 | 4.5 / 5.0 / 5.5 / 6.0 |
| Row 4 | 6.5 \ 7.0 \ 7.5 \ 8.0 |
| Row 5 | 8.5 / 9.0 / 9.5 / 10.0 |

**To solve a story problem, Ben added 3.7 and 2.4.**

**Then he subtracted the sum from 15.**

**Write a story problem Ben could have solved this way.**

10  weigh 5.3 ounces.

A can holding 40  weighs 23.7 ounces.

What is the weight of the empty can?
Tell how you found your answer.

- - - - - - - - - - - - - - - - - - - - - - - - - - - - - - - - - - - -

$$\bigcirc + \bigstar = 6.4$$

$$\bigcirc - \bigstar = 1.0$$

$$\bigcirc = \underline{\hspace{1cm}} \qquad \bigstar = \underline{\hspace{1cm}}$$

List the steps you used to solve the problem.

Compare your steps with a classmate's steps.

Add 2.2 going across.

Add 1.5 going up.

What number is A?

What number is B?

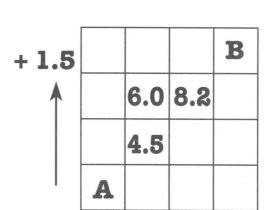

I am a decimal number.

When you add me to 0.5, you get the same answer as when you subtract me from 2.1.

What number am I?

**Think of the names for the numbers 1 through 20.**

- What fraction of the numbers have a name that begins with T?

- What fraction of the number names have fewer than 5 letters?

**Create 2 number-name fraction questions for a classmate to answer.**

**Follow these directions.**

- Color $\frac{1}{4}$ of the rectangle red.
- Color $\frac{1}{5}$ of the rectangle green.
- Color $\frac{1}{20}$ of the rectangle yellow.
- Color the rest of the rectangle blue.

**What fraction of the rectangle is blue?**

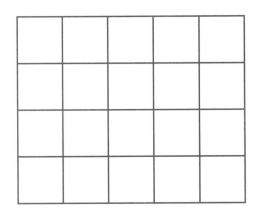

**Which is the greatest?**

one
third
of 60

one
fourth
of 60

one
fifth
of 60

**How did you decide?**

- - - - - - - - - - - - - - - - - - - - - - - - - - - - - - - - - - - - - -

**This is a $+\frac{1}{3}$ pattern.**

**Complete the addition pattern.**

$1, 1\frac{1}{3}, 1\frac{2}{3}, 2, 2\frac{1}{3}$, _____, _____, _____, _____

**This is a $-\frac{1}{3}$ pattern.**

**Complete the subtraction pattern.**

$10, 9\frac{2}{3}, 9\frac{1}{3}, 9, 8\frac{2}{3}$, _____, _____, _____, _____

**Start with any number.**

**Make up a $+\frac{1}{4}$ and a $-\frac{1}{4}$ pattern.**

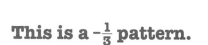

_____, _____, _____, _____, _____, _____, _____, _____

_____, _____, _____, _____, _____, _____, _____, _____

## The fraction is on the sign. Which fraction is it?

- It is greater than $\frac{1}{2}$.
- It is less than $\frac{7}{8}$.
- It is not equal to $\frac{1}{2} + \frac{1}{4}$.

---

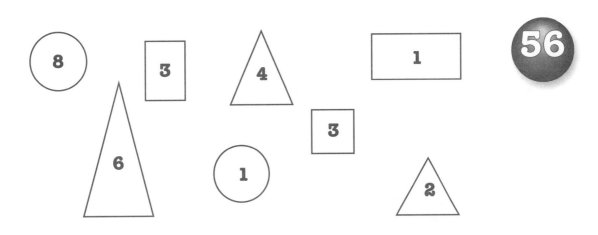

## Here are some game pieces.

- What fraction of the pieces show an even number?
- What fraction of the pieces are circular and show the number 1?
- What fraction of the pieces are not triangular?

**What does the question mark stand for?**

$$\pentagon + 2\frac{2}{3} = 5$$

$$\pentagon - \frac{1}{3} = ?$$

---

Balloons
35¢ each

**Maggie bought $\frac{1}{3}$ of these balloons.**

**What was her change from a 5-dollar bill?**

**Complete the pattern.**

$\frac{1}{4}$, ☐ , $1\frac{1}{4}$, ☐ , ☐ , $2\frac{3}{4}$, $3\frac{1}{4}$, ☐

**What did you add each time to get the next number?**

---

Name a fraction between
- 0 and 1
- 0 and $\frac{1}{2}$
- 0 and $\frac{1}{4}$

Use the clues.

**Find the fraction on the sign.**

**Clues**

- It is less than $\frac{9}{10}$.
- It is greater than $\frac{2}{10}$.
- It is not equal to $\frac{5}{10}$.

**The fraction is ____ .**

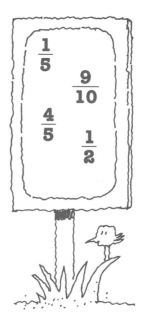

---

**Work with a partner.**

**Each of you write 3 fractions on separate cards or pieces of paper.**

**Then place all of the cards in order from least to greatest.**

**Write the fractions in order.**

**63**

$\frac{2}{3}$ of a mystery number is 18.

What is the mystery number?

**Write a fraction mystery problem.**

**Give it to a classmate to solve.**

- - - - - - - - - - - - - - - - - - - - - - - - - - - - - - - - - - - - - - -

**64**

Charlie's chocolates
$3.99
$\frac{1}{2}$ pound

Finnerty's Finest Chocolates
$15
$1\frac{1}{2}$ pounds

**You like both kinds of chocolates.**

**Which is the better buy?**

**Tell how you know.**

**Solve each problem by naming the coin.**

- $\frac{1}{4}$ of a dollar is a _____ .
- $\frac{1}{10}$ of a dollar is a _____ .
- $\frac{1}{5}$ of a quarter is a _____ .
- $\frac{1}{2}$ of a dime is a _____ .
- $\frac{1}{5}$ of a nickel is a _____ .
- $\frac{1}{2}$ of a dollar is a _____ .

------------------------------------------------------

**Lisa's Day**

Friends $\frac{1}{12}$

Job $\frac{1}{6}$

Sleeping $\frac{1}{3}$

Eating $\frac{1}{12}$

School and Homework $\frac{1}{3}$

**What fraction of her day did Lisa spend eating or with friends?**

**What fraction of her day did she spend awake?**

Think of the numbers 1 to 30.
What fraction of them have a
remainder of 1 when divided by 3?

- - - - - - - - - - - - - - - - - - - - - - - - - - - - - - - - - - - - - - -

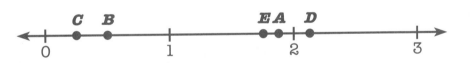

## Match each fraction on the gear to a point on the number line.

- Point *A* is _____ .
- Point *B* is _____ .
- Point *C* is _____ .
- Point *D* is _____ .
- Point *E* is _____ .

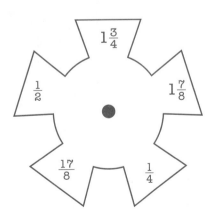

**Which fraction is greater?**

$\frac{5}{8}$     $\frac{7}{12}$

**Explain to a friend how to tell which fraction is greater.**

- - - - - - - - - - - - - - - - - - - - - - - - - - - - - - - - - - - - - - - - - - - -

**You are driving on Highway 7.**

**You are halfway between Center City and Ashford.**

**How many miles are you from Center City?**

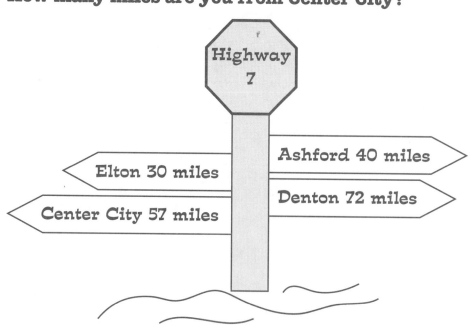

Highway 7

Elton 30 miles

Ashford 40 miles

Denton 72 miles

Center City 57 miles

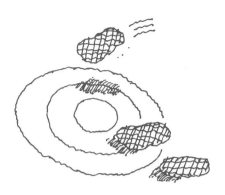

**Carla, Max, and Manfred played a game.**

- Sixty points were scored.
- Manfred scored $\frac{1}{4}$ of the points.
- Carla scored $\frac{1}{3}$ of the points.

**How many points did Max score?**

- - - - - - - - - - - - - - - - - - - - - - - - - - - - - - - - - - - - - - -

**You want to make 36 muffins for a party.**

**Tell how much you need of each ingredient.**

---

### Bran Muffins

| | |
|---|---|
| $1\frac{1}{4}$ c flour | $\frac{1}{4}$ t nutmeg |
| 1 c bran | $\frac{1}{4}$ c milk |
| 1 T baking powder | 1 c oil |
| $\frac{3}{4}$ t cinnamon | 1 egg |

*Makes 1 dozen muffins*

---

**You are thinking of the fraction $\frac{5}{8}$.**

**You want your friend to name your fraction with 3 clues.**

**Make up a third clue.**

**Clues**

1. The fraction is more than $\frac{1}{2}$.
2. The fraction is less than $\frac{3}{4}$.
3.

73

---

**Joshua collects stamps from South America.**

- He has 250 stamps
- Half of his stamps are from Brazil.
- One tenth of the stamps are from Venezuela.
- The rest of the stamps are from Peru.

**Joshua keeps the stamps in an album with 10 stamps on each page.**

**The pages are organized by country.**

**How many pages are needed for the stamps from Peru?**

74

**There were 60 questions on the history test.**

**Gerald got $\frac{4}{5}$ of the first 20 questions correct.**

**He got $\frac{9}{10}$ of the remaining questions correct.**

**How many questions did Gerald get correct altogether?**

---

The difference of two fractions is $\frac{1}{18}$.

One of the fractions is $\frac{2}{9}$.

What is the other fraction?

Is there another answer?

**Jeff had $6.00.**

- He spent $\frac{1}{2}$ of his money on a magazine.
- He spent $\frac{2}{3}$ of what he had left for lunch.
- He spent 60¢ for bus fare home.

**How much money did Jeff have left?**

- - - - - - - - - - - - - - - - - - - - - - - - - - - - - - - - - - - - - - -

**I am thinking of two fractions.**

- When you add them, their sum is 1.
- When you subtract them, their difference is 0.

**What are the fractions?**

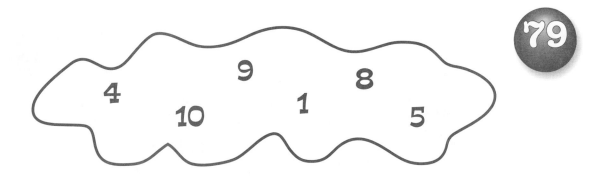

**Use each number from the cloud once.**

- A fraction that is equivalent to $\frac{1}{2}$ is $\dfrac{\Box}{\Box}$.

- The greatest proper fraction you can write is $\dfrac{\Box}{\Box}$.

- A fraction less than $\frac{1}{2}$ is $\dfrac{\Box}{\Box}$.

- - - - - - - - - - - - - - - - - - - - - - - - - - - - - - - - - -

**Put 12 pennies in a bag and shake them.**

- Spill the pennies onto a desk or table.
- Write a fraction to tell how many of the pennies landed heads up.
- Do this 5 times.

**Order the fractions from least to greatest.**

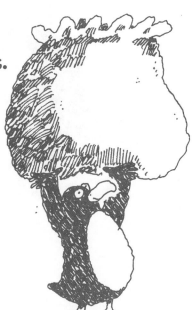

**81**

Three fourths of a
number is 15.
What is one fourth of
the same number?
How do you know?

- - - - - - - - - - - - - - - - - - - - - - - - - - - - - - - - -

**82**

What fraction of the
numbers from 200
through 400 are
multiples of 10?

**What is the start number?**

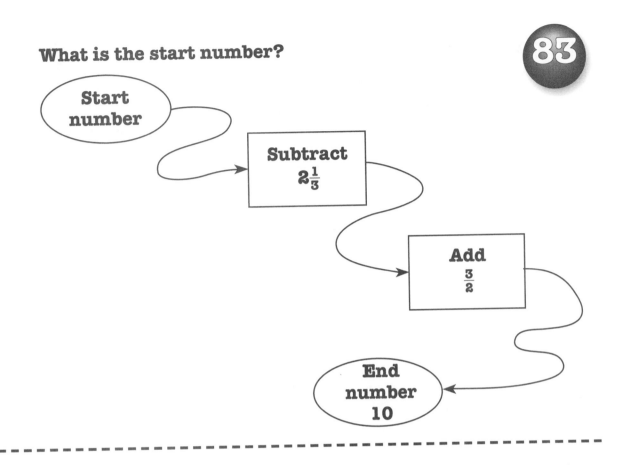

Start
number

Subtract
$2\frac{1}{3}$

Add
$\frac{3}{2}$

End
number
10

- - - - - - - - - - - - - - - - - - - - - - - - - - - - - - - - - - - - - - - - - - -

$1\frac{1}{2}$

6                    33        $5\frac{1}{2}$        9

90

**Use the numbers shown.**

**Fill in the blanks so that the story makes sense.**

Each day, Luke walks for _____ hours, or
_____ minutes.

He walks _____ miles.

Luke walks _____ days each week, for a total
of _____ hours and _____ miles.

**This morning I had some marbles.**

- I gave $\frac{1}{2}$ of the marbles to a friend.
- I lost $\frac{1}{2}$ of the marbles I had left.
- I now have 15 marbles.

**How many marbles did I have this morning?**

---

 86

**Deli Special**

*This week only*

**Swiss Cheese**
**$5.60 per pound**

**Rubin uses about $\frac{1}{8}$ of a pound of Swiss cheese to make 1 sandwich.**

**How much did Rubin pay for cheese to make 10 sandwiches?**

**List the steps you used to find the cost.**

**Use all of the fractions on the pyramid.**

**Write one fraction in each ☐ to make the statements true.**

$$\boxed{\phantom{x}} = \boxed{\phantom{x}} \qquad \boxed{\phantom{x}} > \boxed{\phantom{x}} > \boxed{\phantom{x}}$$

---

If  is equal to 3,

what does each piece below equal?

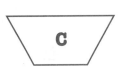

**Start with any fraction.**

- Add $\frac{3}{4}$.

- Subtract $\frac{1}{8}$.

- Subtract $\frac{5}{8}$.

**What do you notice about the last fraction?**

**Try a different starting fraction.**

**Why do you think this happens?**

---

**Four friends went shopping.**

- Tamika spent $\frac{1}{2}$ of a dollar.
- Rosa spent $\frac{3}{4}$ of a dollar.
- Ken spent $1\frac{1}{4}$ dollars.
- Jamie spent $1\frac{1}{2}$ dollars.

**Altogether, how much less than $5 did they spend?**

**What is half of a half of a half of 80?**

**Josua has a box of blocks.**

- $\frac{1}{4}$ of the blocks are green.
- $\frac{1}{4}$ of the blocks are red.
- 10 of the blocks are blue.

**How many blocks are in the box?**

$\frac{2}{5}$ of the letters in this word are vowels.

# D R I V E

**Write a word to fit each clue.**

- Clue A: $\frac{1}{4}$ of the letters are the same.
- Clue B: $\frac{4}{5}$ of the letters are consonants.
- Clue C: $\frac{1}{6}$ of the letters are T.

**Suppose you compared your word for a clue with those of your classmates.**

**Would the words all have to have the same number of letters? Why or why not?**

---

**Alex says she can prove that $\frac{1}{2} + \frac{1}{2} = \frac{1}{2}$.**

1 and 1 is 2.

2 and 2 is 4.

That means $\frac{1}{2} + \frac{1}{2} = \frac{2}{4}$.

$\frac{2}{4}$ is another name for $\frac{1}{2}$.

So $\frac{1}{2} + \frac{1}{2} = \frac{1}{2}$.

**What's wrong with Alex's thinking?**

**I have $2 in quarters, nickels, and dimes in my bank.**

- One half of the coins are quarters.
- One third of the coins are dimes.
- One sixth of the coins are nickels.

**How many of each coin do I have?**

_____ quarters    _____ dimes    _____ nickels

**Check: Is the total value of the coins $2?**

---

10    6         8    12    96

         5

    4              2

**Use all of the numbers above to write equivalent fractions.**

$$\frac{1}{\bigstar} = \frac{\bigstar}{\bigstar} = \frac{\bigstar}{\bigstar} = \frac{\bigstar}{\bigstar}$$

**Work with a partner.**

**Each partner lists a set of 9 numbers that fits the facts.**

**Facts**

- $\frac{1}{3}$ of the numbers are odd.

- $\frac{1}{3}$ of the numbers are multiples of 5.

- $\frac{2}{3}$ of the numbers are multiples of 3.

**Exchange sets.**

**Check your partner's set.**

**Does it fit the facts?**

Half of a half of a half of some number is 4. What is the number?

**Use these numbers to complete the magic square.**

$0 \qquad \frac{7}{12} \qquad \frac{1}{12} \qquad \frac{1}{2} \qquad \frac{1}{6} \qquad \frac{1}{4} \qquad \frac{2}{3}$

**The sum of each row, column, and diagonal must be 1.**

**Magic Square**

| | | $\frac{5}{12}$ |
|---|---|---|
| | $\frac{1}{3}$ | |
| | | |

**Compare your magic square with those of classmates.**

**Are they the same?**

- - - - - - - - - - - - - - - - - - - - - - - - - - - - - - - - - - - - - - - -

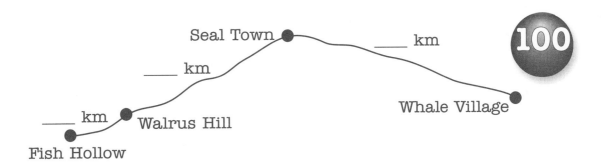

Seal Town

_____ km

_____ km

Whale Village

_____ km

Walrus Hill

Fish Hollow

**Write the distances between each pair of cities on the map.**

- The distance from Fish Hollow to Walrus Hill is $\frac{1}{3}$ the distance from Walrus Hill to Seal Town.

- The distance from Fish Hollow to Walrus Hill is $\frac{1}{4}$ the distance from Seal Town to Whale Village.

- It is 51 kilometers from Walrus Hill to Seal Town.

# Answers

1. The missing numbers are 8.3, 8.9, 9.5, and 10.7. Pattern: Each decimal, after 6.5, is 0.6 more than the decimal before.

2. 0.4, 1.2, 0.2, 0.5, 1.9

3. Miki: 5.8; Leah: 4.9; Kim: 6.0; Craig: 4.2

4. more than 1.01 in.

5. Answers will vary.

6. 0.4 or 0.40

7. $300

8. Answers will vary.

9. week 3, 3.5 cm

10. 1.8

11. 401.23

12. 6.3, 4.4

13. Possible set: 0.5, 1.2, 1.3, 1.4, 1.8, 2.2

14.

| | | |
|---|---|---|
| 7.1 | 2.3 | (9.4) |
| 1.2 | 5.7 | (6.9) |
| 6.9 | 0.1 | (7.0) |
| (15.2) | (8.1) | |

15. 216 km

16. yes; Possible explanation: Rounding up, 3 bags of chips cost $3, and 2 granola bars cost $4; a total of $7, which is less than $8.

17. from top to bottom: Joy, Nita, Sean, Mai

18. terms 6, 11, 16, and 21

19. Subtract 2.1

21. 7.63 – 2.54

22. 4.8

23. 60¢, or $.60; 90¢, or $.90

24. Answers will vary.

25. 8 or 8.0

26. No; ticket 10 has the number 3.9, ticket 12 has the number 4.5.

27.
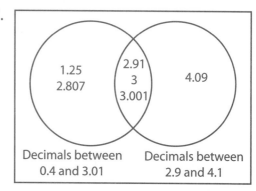

28. 57.6 and 36.6; 2.459 and 14.84; 0.4 and 0.75

29. 4.6, 4.09, 4.59, $\frac{47}{10}$

30. 25.2 mi

31. 6.6 oz; Possible explanation: 3 spheres are 5.4 × 3 = 16.2 oz, so 2 pyramids are 29.4 – 16.2 = 13.2 oz, so 1 pyramid is 13.2 ÷ 2 = 6.6 oz.

32. 7:35 P.M.

33. 6.5, 4.25, 2.25, 2.1, 3.6

34. 2.45, 2.54, 4.25, 4.52, 5.24, 5.42

35. 10.25, 7.25

36. 12.45 + 3.21 = 15.66, 4.57 + 3.43 = 8

37.

| | | | |
|---|---|---|---|
| 0.9 | 11.5 | 6.9 | (19.3) |
| 3.8 | 9.7 | 7.4 | (20.9) |
| 6.2 | 0.3 | 2.6 | (9.1) |
| (10.9) | (21.5) | (16.9) | |

38. Possible explanation: The answer to A is 1.36. Since 2.56 is 0.20 more to take away, the difference in B will be 0.20 less than 1.36, or 1.16.

39. 1.5 oz

40. $8.9 + 3.4 = 12.3$ (or $3.4 + 8.9 = 12.3$), $7.5 - 2.7 = 4.8$, $5 \times 4.6 = 23$ (or $4.6 \times 5 = 23$)

41. 3.4 km; Questions will vary.

42. 3.2 cm

43. There are several possible answers; one is $5.4 > 3.2 > 1.0$.

44. Answers will vary.

45. 40.5; Explanations will vary.

46. Story problems will vary.

47. 2.5 oz; Explanations will vary.

48. 3.7, 2.7; Explanations will vary.

49. $A = 0.8, B = 11.9$

50. 0.8

51. $\frac{6}{20}$ or $\frac{3}{10}, \frac{7}{20}$; Questions will vary.

52. $\frac{10}{20}$ or $\frac{1}{2}$

53. one third of 60; Explanations will vary.

54. $2\frac{2}{3}, 3, 3\frac{1}{3}, 3\frac{2}{3}; 8\frac{1}{3}, 8, 7\frac{2}{3}, 7\frac{1}{3}$; Patterns will vary.

55. $\frac{5}{8}$

56. $\frac{4}{8}$ or $\frac{1}{2}, \frac{1}{8}, \frac{5}{8}$

57. 2

58. $3.60

59. The missing numbers are $\frac{3}{4}, 1\frac{3}{4}, 2\frac{1}{4}$, and $3\frac{3}{4}$. Each time, $\frac{2}{4}$ or $\frac{1}{2}$ is added.

60. Answers will vary.

61. $\frac{4}{5}$

62. Answers will vary.

63. 27; Problems will vary.

64. Charlie's; Possible explanation: At $3.99 for a half pound, $1\frac{1}{2}$ lb is $3 \times \$3.99$, or about $12, which is less than $15.

65. quarter, dime, nickel, nickel, penny, half dollar

66. $\frac{2}{12}$ or $\frac{1}{6}, \frac{8}{12}$ or $\frac{2}{3}$

67. $\frac{10}{30}$ or $\frac{1}{3}$

68. $1\frac{7}{8}, \frac{1}{2}, \frac{1}{4}, \frac{17}{8}, 1\frac{3}{4}$

69. $\frac{5}{8}$; Possible explanation: Find a common denominator and write equivalent fractions: $\frac{5}{8} = \frac{15}{24}$ and $\frac{7}{12} = \frac{14}{24}$. Since $15 > 14, \frac{5}{8} > \frac{7}{12}$.

70. $48\frac{1}{2}$ mi

71. 25 points

72. $3\frac{3}{4}$ c flour, 3 c bran, 3 T baking powder, $2\frac{1}{4}$ t cinnamon, $\frac{3}{4}$ t nutmeg, $\frac{3}{4}$ c milk, 3 c oil, 3 eggs

73. Possible clue: The denominator is 8.

74. 10 pages

75. 52 questions

76. There are two answers: $\frac{3}{18}$ or $\frac{1}{6}$, and $\frac{5}{18}$.

77. 40¢

78. $\frac{1}{2}$ and $\frac{1}{2}$ (or other fractions equivalent to $\frac{1}{2}$)

79. $\frac{4}{8}, \frac{9}{10}, \frac{1}{5}$

80. Answers will vary.

81. 5; Explanations will vary.

82. $\frac{21}{201}$

83. $10\frac{5}{6}$

84. $1\frac{1}{2}, 90, 5\frac{1}{2}, 6, 9, 33$

85. 60 marbles

86. $7; Steps will vary.

87. $\frac{2}{5} = \frac{4}{10}, \frac{3}{5} > \frac{1}{2} > \frac{2}{10}$

88. $A = 1, B = \frac{1}{2}, C = 1\frac{1}{2}$

89. The ending and starting fractions are equivalent. Subtracting $\frac{1}{8}$ and $\frac{5}{8}$ (a total of $\frac{6}{8}$, or $\frac{3}{4}$) undoes adding $\frac{3}{4}$.

90. $1 less

91. 10

92. 20 blocks

93. Words will vary. No; explanations will vary.

94. She added the numerators and the denominators when, since the denominators are the same, she should have added the numerators only.

95. 6, 4, 2

96. $\frac{1}{2} = \frac{4}{8} = \frac{5}{10} = \frac{6}{12}$ (The order of the last three fractions is not important.)

97. Possible set that fits the facts: 2, 3, 5, 15, 4, 6, 12, 24, 30

98. 32

99. Possible magic square:

| $\frac{1}{12}$ | $\frac{1}{2}$ | $\frac{5}{12}$ |
|---|---|---|
| $\frac{2}{3}$ | $\frac{1}{3}$ | 0 |
| $\frac{1}{4}$ | $\frac{1}{6}$ | $\frac{7}{12}$ |

Magic squares do not have to match.

100. From left to right: 17 km, 51 km, 68 km